SCHIRMER'S LIBRARY
OF MUSICAL CLASSICS

Vol. 1964

WOLFGANG AMADEUS MOZART

Violin Sonata
In A Major, K. 526

For Violin an Piano

Edited by
RAFAEL DRUIAN and RUDOLF FIRKUŠNÝ

ISBN 978-1-4950-1144-3

G. SCHIRMER, Inc.

DISTRIBUTED BY

HAL•LEONARD®
CORPORATION
7777 W. BLUEMOUND RD. P.O. BOX 13819 MILWAUKEE, WI 53213

www.musicsalesclassical.com
www.halleonard.com

Sonata
[K. 526]

W. A. MOZART
Composed in August, 1787, at Vienna

81

87

92

98

104

142

148

154

160

166

198

204

210

216

221

Recommended syncopation:

Violin

Sonata

[K. 526]

W. A. MOZART

Molto allegro (c ♩. = 120 126)

✔ = slight separation
Ⓡ = bow retrieve
All markings in parenthesis are editorial suggestions.

Violin

a) Notes marked with the sign ı
should be played as long
expressive but separate notes.

Violin

a) The separate ♩ as well as the separate ♪ in this movement should be played off the string. b) see m. 5   c) See m.25.
d) Near the frog.

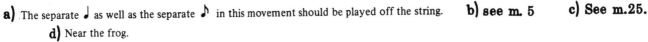

Violin

5

a) Near the frog.   b) See note a), p.4.

Violin

a) The trills should start with the upper note on the beat. **b)** **c)** **d) Near the frog.**

Violin

a) Near the frog.   **b)**

Violin

19

97

103

109

115

121

160

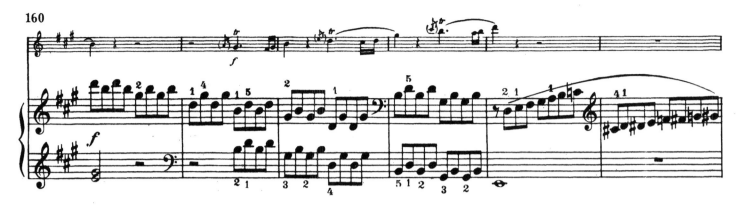

166

172

179

186

193

198

203

208

213

219

224

229

234

239

274

279

284

289

295

301

307

313

319

324

330

336

343

349

354

360

367

374

381

387